ANATOMY OF AN ASSASSINATION

101 Things You Didn't Know About the Killing of John F. Kennedy

By Horace Martin Woodhouse
Author of *Executive Privilege*

COPYRIGHT NOTICE

Anatomy of an Assassination: 101 Things You Didn't Know About the Killing of John F. Kennedy is published and copyrighted © 2013 by History Company, LLC (www.historycompany.com). All rights reserved. No part of this book may be reproduced in any form by any electronic or mechanical means (including photocopying, recording, or information storage or retrieval) without permission in writing from the publisher. Users are not permitted to mount any part of this book on the World Wide Web. Requests to the publisher for permission should be addressed to the Permissions Department, History Company LLC, 373 Enfield Falls Road, Ithaca, NY 14850.

Limit of Liability/Disclaimer of Warranty: While the publisher and the author have used their best efforts in preparing this book, they make no representations or warranties with respect to the accuracy or completeness of the contents of this book. No warranty may be created or extended by sales representatives or written sales materials. Neither the publisher nor the author shall be liable for any loss of profit or any other commercial damages, including but not limited to special, incidental, consequential, or other damages resulting from the use of the information contained herein.

History Company books are available at special discounts for bulk purchases of 12 units or more (shipping and handling charges apply). For more information, contact:

History Company LLC
373 Enfield Falls Road, Ithaca, NY 14850
(800) 891-0466

Printed in the United States of America

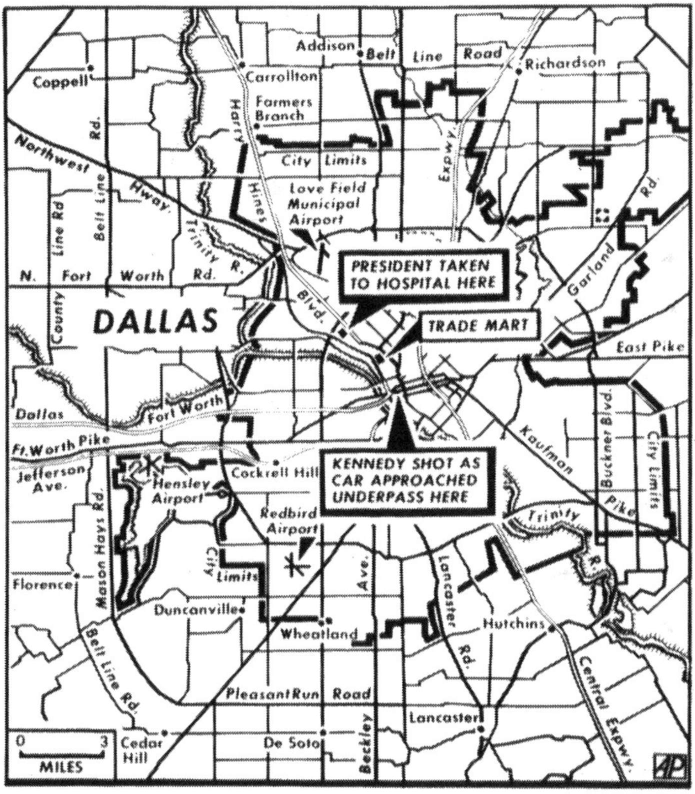

Addison
Belt Line Road
Richardson
Coppell
Carrollton
Farmers Branch
Harry Hines Blvd.
Belt Line Rd.
Northwest Hway.
City Limits
Love Field Municipal Airport
Expwy.
Garland Rd.
County Line Rd
Belt Line
Trinity R.
N. Fort Worth Rd.
PRESIDENT TAKEN TO HOSPITAL HERE
DALLAS
TRADE MART
East Pike
Dallas Fort Worth
Ft. Worth Pike
Jefferson Ave.
Cockrell Hill
KENNEDY SHOT AS CAR APPROACHED UNDERPASS HERE
Kaufman Pike
Buckner Blvd.
City Limits
Hensley Airport
Mason Hays Rd.
Redbird Airport
Trinity R.
City Limits
Ave.
Lancaster Rd.
Florence
Duncanville
Wheatland
Hutchins
Belt Line Rd.
Central Expwy.
Pleasant Run Road
Lancaster
0 3 MILES
Cedar Hill
De Soto
Beckley
AP

> "Things do not happen.
> Things are made to happen."
>
> — John F. Kennedy

Half a century has passed since the fall of 1963, when President Kennedy and his political advisers began preparing for the following year's presidential campaign and the challenges he would face in the South. Although he had not formally announced his candidacy, it was clear that he was going to run and he seemed confident about his chances for re-election. Aware that a feud among party leaders in Texas could jeopardize his chances of carrying the state, the President and First Lady departed on Air Force One for a two-day, five-city tour of Texas.

Arriving at Love Field in Dallas on November 22nd, President and Mrs. Kennedy disembarked and immediately walked toward a fence where a crowd of well-wishers had gathered, and they spent several minutes shaking hands. The First Lady received a bouquet of red roses, which she brought with her to the waiting limousine. That day was destined to become one of the most infamous days in American history.

Considering the magnitude of the event and the government's attempt to blame a lone gunman, it is astonishing that a clear majority of Americans suspect there was a conspiracy behind the killing of the President. Since the passage of fifty years has obscured so much about what happened that day, it's finally time to shed fresh light on this American nightmare. There's a whole book worth of things we know now that we didn't know then. You're holding that book in your hands.

Anatomy of an Assassination is brimming with amazing true stories, corrected myths, and particular particulars about the greatest unsolved crime of the twentieth century. It's not meant to provide a comprehensive nor complete academic reference, but rather an accessible guide to the obscure, the absurd, and sometimes perverse.

Horace Martin Woodhouse

Premonition

In June 1961, President Kennedy's secretary was clearing his table when a slip of paper fell to the floor. She picked it up and the words, in Kennedy's handwriting stated: "I know that there is a God and I see a storm coming. If he has a place for me, I am ready."

Chiefs on the Warpath

Kennedy had an uncomfortable relationship with the Joint Chiefs of Staff – particularly Air Force General Curtis LeMay – who were unhappy with what they considered his tentative approach to the Soviets and who wanted to maximize America's window of nuclear superiority. In *JFK's Last Hundred Days*, Thurston Clarke writes that "by the fall of 1962 the President not only believed a coup was possible, but had reportedly discussed its likelihood." Kennedy urged director John Frankenheimer to make a film of "Seven Days in May," the coup-plotted best seller by Fletcher Knebel and Charles Bailey. (The film came out in 1964.)

Assassination Vacation

During the Cuban Missile Crisis, General Curtis LeMay called Kennedy an appeaser – equivalent to Neville Chamberlain – for not bombing Cuba. LeMay's official biography indicates that at the time of the assassination he was on vacation, hunting and fishing with family members in upstate Michigan. But an Andrews Air Force base log book indicates that LeMay ordered a special Air Force jet to pick him up in Canada shortly after news of the assassination was widely broadcast, which indicated to some that he wasn't hunting and fishing in Michigan. Although there should be a more thorough record in government archives to document the whereabouts of the general, it's not known for certain where he was at the time of the assassination nor where he went after he arrived in Washington.

Most Wanted

Anti-Kennedy handbills were placed on car windshields and tucked inside racks of the two Dallas daily newspapers the day before the President's arrival. These handbills simulated a "man wanted" police placard with a reproduction of a front and profile photograph of the President and listed a series of inflammatory charges against him, the creation of Robert Surrey, an associate of ultra-conservative retired Major General Edwin Walker.

Uniquely Insecure

In flagrant violation of Secret Service regulations, nine of the agents guarding President Kennedy in Dallas (including four in the escort car behind the presidential limousine) had been out drinking until the early hours on the morning of November 22nd at a nightclub called The Cellar. It was part of a disturbing pattern of similar misbehavior by the White House detail – a pattern that materially increased the possibility of an assassination attempt succeeding. As a result, escort security for the motorcade was, in the words of the House Assassinations Committee, "uniquely insecure."

Counterfeit Detail

The assassination of President Kennedy was the first and only such crime since the Secret Service was assigned responsibility for full-time protection of the President in 1901, as a result of the assassination of William McKinley. When originally formed in 1865, the agency was not responsible for presidential protection, even though that was the year Lincoln was murdered. Its primary purpose was to deal with counterfeiting, which had become rampant following the Civil War. The Secret Service then evolved into a domestic intelligence and counterintelligence agency.

In the Line of Duty

Roy Herman Kellerman joined the Secret Service in 1941, transferring to the White House detail the following year. As the agent in charge of the Texas trip, Kellerman was riding in the front passenger seat of the presidential limousine. At about 12:30 PM the car entered Elm Street. Soon afterwards a shot was fired. Like all Secret Service agents assigned to protect the president, Kellerman was trained to use his own body as a shield, taking a bullet if necessary in the line of duty. Kellerman took no action to cover the president with his body, although it would have been consistent with Secret Service procedure for him to have done so.

Widow's Tale

After President Kennedy's assassination, Agent Kellerman was promoted, retiring from the Secret Service in 1968 as an assistant administrator. He died in St. Petersburg, Florida, on March 22, 1984, of unreported causes. According to his widow, June, Kellerman believed the murder of John F. Kennedy was a conspiracy.

Covering the Body

Secret Service agent Rufus Youngblood was riding with Lyndon Johnson, two cars behind the presidential limousine. According to Youngblood, when the first shot rang out he didn't know whether the sound he heard was a firecracker, a bomb or a gunshot. He only knew that something was wrong and that some action had to be taken. Youngblood scrambled over the seat, pushed Johnson to the floor and spread his own body protectively on top of the Vice President. As it turned out, Johnson was never in real danger from the gunfire trained on the President.

Clear and Present Danger

Agent Clint Hill was riding in the car directly behind the presidential limousine when the attack began. While the shooting continued, Hill leapt from the running board of the car he was riding on and jumped onto the back of the President's moving car. As he got on, Mrs. Kennedy, apparently in shock, was crawling onto the flat rear trunk of the moving limousine (he later told the Warren Commission that he thought Mrs. Kennedy was reaching for a piece of the President's skull which had been blown off). Agent Hill crawled to her and guided the First Lady back into her seat. Although the Secret Service was shocked at its failure to protect the life of the President, virtually everyone agreed that Hill's rapid and brave actions had been without blemish. He was honored at a ceremony in Washington just days after the President's funeral. Mrs. Kennedy, despite being in deep mourning, made a rare appearance at this same event to thank him in person.

Eye of the Storm

Dealey Plaza is a Dallas city park on land donated by Dallas philanthropist Sarah Horton Cockrell, completed in 1940 as a WPA project on the west edge of downtown Dallas where three streets converge (Main Street, Elm Street, and Commerce Street) to pass under a railroad bridge known locally as the triple underpass. The plaza is named for George Bannerman Dealey, an early publisher of the *The Dallas Morning News* and civic leader, and the man who had campaigned for the area's revitalization.

Road to Ruin

The route of the presidential motorcade, violating Secret Service protocol by involving turns of 90 and 120 degrees, was strongly criticized by former DNC advance man Marty Underwood and former uniformed Secret Service agent John Norris. The presidential limousine entered Dealey Plaza, moved slowly along Houston Street, then took a left turn right in front of the Texas School Book Depository building. A diagram of the route was printed in the *Dallas Times Herald* on November 19th – a practice the Secret Service halted in the wake of the assassination. Secret Service Chief James J. Rowley adamantly denied that his agency was responsible for the newspaper printing of the Dallas motorcade route.

Bystanders

While watching the motorcade in Dealey Plaza, bystander Arnold Rowland and his wife observed two men and what appeared to be a rifle in the east corner window on the sixth floor of the School Book Depository at approximately 12:15 PM. He commented to his wife that they must be Secret Service agents. There were, of course, no agents in the building.

"Let's Get Out of Here!"

After working for over a decade as a chauffeur to several wealthy families, including the Lodge family, William Robert Greer became a Secret Service agent. As driver of the presidential limousine in the motorcade through Dealey Plaza, Greer has been criticized for his actions during the assassination, noting that he did not accelerate the vehicle to get the President out of danger as soon as he could have. After the first shot was fired, agent Roy Kellerman shouted to Greer, "Let's get out of here," however, Greer hits the breaks. More bullets were fired and Kennedy was hit in the head. In the confusion after the first shot was fired, the limousine's brake lights can be seen coming on briefly, slowing the car to almost a walking pace. The vehicle accelerated several seconds later, but by then the fatal shot had been fired. Since that time, Secret Service drivers have been trained to accelerate rapidly out of the area if they even think they hear gunfire.

Naming Rights

The small, sloping hill inside Dealey Plaza that became infamous following the assassination was first called the "grassy knoll" by reporter Albert Merriman Smith of UPI, in his second dispatch from the radio-telephone in the press car: "Some of the Secret Service agents thought the gunfire was from an automatic weapon fired to the right rear of the President's car, probably from a grassy knoll to which police rushed." The term was repeated by other reporters for several hours until investigators became convinced the shots originated from the Texas School Book Depository. Yet it remains an historical fact that police and spectators immediately ran to the grassy knoll, not to the Depository. In 1964, Smith won the Pulitzer Prize for his coverage of the assassination, and "grassy knoll" has become a modern slang expression indicating suspicion, conspiracy, or a cover-up.

Ghost Riders

Although presidential motorcades on prior stops during the Texas trip included anywhere from three to six motorcyclists on each side of the President's limousine (a fact confirmed by numerous press and official White House films and photographs), the plans for Dallas were altered by Secret Service officials to give President Kennedy just four non-flanking outriders. The origin of the order to strip presidential security by reducing motorcycle-based security remains mysterious, and carries sinister implications.

Love and Death

As the motorcade moved through the cheering crowds in Dallas, Nellie Connally, wife of the Texas governor, leaned over to the President and exclaimed, "You can't say Dallas doesn't love you!" Then the shots rang out.

Missed Calls

In Washington, D.C. there was an astonishing breakdown of communications when the telephone system in the nation's capital went out almost immediately upon reports of the shooting. The Chesapeake & Potomac's Friday record of over a quarter-million long-distance calls was staggering, a phenomenon communications engineers call "the slow dial tone," a result of overloaded exchanges. Lines would go dead, return to normal when a sufficient number of people had hung up, and go dead again and return to life, over and over. The pattern was repeated throughout the country.

Tricky Dick

Richard Nixon, the man who had lost to Kennedy in the 1960 presidential campaign, was in Dallas on November 22nd to attend a Pepsi-Cola board meeting, representing the company's law firm (Mudge, Rose, Nixon et al). As the session was breaking up, news of the assassination came through. Nixon returned to his hotel and later in the afternoon was driven to the Dallas airport by a Pepsi Cola official. For some reason, the timeline of Nixon's visit to Dallas has always been deliberately obscured, in particular by Nixon himself. He claimed he first heard the news from a cabbie when he arrived back in New York.

Memo of Understanding

On the day of Kennedy's funeral, November 25, 1963, a memorandum sent from Assistant Attorney General Katzenbach to Bill Moyers, press secretary to the newly sworn-in President Johnson, states, "The public must be satisfied that Oswald was the assassin; that he did not have confederates who are still at large; and that evidence was such that he would have been convicted at trial." The Warren Commission was created four days later.

Act of Commission

On November 29, 1963, President Johnson signed Executive Order 11130 creating a commission headed by Supreme Court Chief Justice Earl Warren. Soon dubbed the Warren Commission, this body's other members included Senators Russell and Cooper, Representatives Ford and Boggs, John McCloy, and Allen Dulles. The commissioners took the testimony of about 100 witnesses, starting with Lee Oswald's wife Marina on February 3, 1964. The staff lawyers interviewed hundreds more, in Washington and in other cities including Dallas and New Orleans. The FBI also conducted thousands of interviews on behalf of the Commission.

Fool on the Hill

John Jay McCloy served as Assistant Secretary of War during World War II, president of the World Bank, U.S. High Commissioner for Germany, chairman of Chase Manhattan Bank, and chairman of the Council on Foreign Relations. He later became a prominent presidential advisor, a member of the foreign policy establishment group of elders called "The Wise Men," and served on the Warren Commission. Notably, he was initially skeptical of the lone gunman theory, but a trip to Dallas with CIA veteran Allen Dulles, the most active member of the Commission, convinced him of the case against Oswald. (Dulles had nothing but scorn for critical arguments against the Oswald-did-it hypothesis; his appointment has been criticized by some historians, who have noted that Kennedy fired him from the CIA, and he was therefore unlikely to be impartial or objective).

Bogged Down

One of the Warren Commission members who later became its biggest critic was Congressman Hale Boggs. In his words, "We have not been told the truth about Oswald." In 1972, his plane went missing in Alaska and he and the pilot were never heard from again. The events surrounding Boggs' death have been the subject of much speculation, suspicion, and numerous conspiracy theories. Boggs dissented from the Warren Commission's majority who supported the single bullet theory. Regarding the single-bullet theory, he said, "I had strong doubts about it."

Greatest Hoax

One of the most tantalizing nuggets about Richard Nixon's possible inside knowledge of the Kennedy assassination secrets was buried on a White House tape until 2002. On the tape, recorded in May of 1972, the President confided to two top aides that the Warren Commission pulled off "the greatest hoax that has ever been perpetuated."

Up to Snuff

At the conclusion of a 1976 investigation into how the Commission was served by the FBI and CIA, Senator Richard Schweiker stated on national television that "the John F. Kennedy assassination investigation was snuffed out before it even began," and that "the fatal mistake the Warren Commission made was to not use its own investigators, but instead to rely on the CIA and FBI personnel, which played directly into the hands of senior intelligence officials who directed the cover-up."

Innocent Bystander

While President Kennedy was the only mortality on November 22nd, Texas Governor John Connally was apparently not the only person wounded that day. James Tague, standing atop the triple overpass, sustained a hit to the cheek by the fragments of either a bullet or concrete knocked loose by a bullet. The impact opened a tiny wound on his cheek, sufficient to do little more than draw a drop of blood. There is no consensus on which bullet could have directly or indirectly caused the scratch. In fact, including the shot that missed and injured James Tague, an absolute minimum of six shots had to have been fired during the assassination.

Chip Off the Block

Upon examination of the area where James Tague had been standing, the upper part of the Main Street south curb, detectives discovered a "very fresh scar" impact that looked like a bullet had struck there and removed a small chip out of the curb's concrete. They came to the conclusion that a bullet ricocheted off the curb and the debris hit Tague. The curb surrounding the scar chip was cut out in August 1964, repaired with a foreign-material patch, and was placed in the National Archives. No documented authorization exists of precisely who or what agency had the scar chip within its evidence chain, nor when or why the chip was covered up.

Brief Encounter

After shots rang out in Dealey Plaza, NBC White House correspondent Robert MacNeil, who was with the presidential motorcade, jumped out of one of the press cars and ran up the grassy knoll with a crowd that was chasing a suspected assassin. After observing the situation on the knoll, MacNeil walked back up Elm Street to the entrance of the School Book Depository, where, upon entering, asked a man for the nearest telephone; the man pointed and went on his way. MacNeil later learned the man he encountered was Lee Harvey Oswald. (MacNeil later paired with Jim Lehrer to create *The MacNeil/Lehrer Report* on PBS).

The Good Wife

Marina Nikolayevna Prusakova met Lee Harvey Oswald, a former U.S. Marine who had defected to the Soviet Union, at a dance on March 17, 1961. They married on April 30, 1961 and in June, the Oswalds returned to the United States and settled in Dallas. Marina learned of the assassination of President Kennedy following the massive media coverage that commenced within minutes of the event, and later, the arrest of her husband. That afternoon, Dallas Police Department detectives arrived at their home, and when asked if Lee owned a rifle, Marina gestured to the garage, where Lee stored his rifle rolled up in a blanket. When detectives unfurled the blanket, no rifle was found. In 1965, Marina married Kenneth Jess Porter, with whom she has two sons. She contends that Oswald was innocent of the assassination.

This Byrd Has Flown

David Harold Byrd, a conservative business tycoon who had close relationships with Lyndon Johnson, John Connally, and George H. W. Bush, was the owner of the Texas School Book Depository building. In November, 1963, Byrd left Texas to go on a two-month safari in Africa. While he was away, Kennedy was assassinated; Lee Harvey Oswald, who was accused of being the lone-gunman, worked in Byrd's Book Depository. Soon after Byrd's return, President Lyndon Johnson, granted a large defense contract his company to build fighter planes (the A-7 Corsair II).

Support and Defend

Lyndon Johnson was sworn in as President by Judge Sarah T. Hughes just hours after the assassination. Judge Hughes brought a small bible for the swearing-in ceremony, but it was replaced with a Roman Missal (a book containing all the prayers and responses necessary for celebrating the mass throughout the year) that was found on the plane. Previously, only two other presidents did not use a bible when taking the oath – Theodore Roosevelt in 1901 and John Quincy Adams who swore on a book of law, with the intention that he was swearing on the constitution.

Lies and Liars

Dallas police officer J. D. Tippit was supposedly shot and killed by Lee Harvey Oswald after Tippit stopped Oswald for questioning, about 45 minutes after the assassination. Oswald's initial arrest was for Tippit's murder, not Kennedy's. According to some Warren Commission critics, Oswald was set up to be killed by Tippit, but Tippit was killed by Oswald before he could carry out his assignment. Other critics doubt that Tippit was killed by Oswald and assert he was shot by other conspirators. Attorney Sterling Harwood suggests that Tippit must have had a role in a conspiracy to kill Kennedy or to silence Oswald, since there is no other reason for an experienced officer like Tippit to fail to call in to his dispatcher his spotting of a suspect fitting the description of Kennedy's killer before engaging the suspect. The only witness to the Tippit shooting, Aquilla Clemmons, claimed she saw two men involved in the shooting. None of her two descriptions matched Oswald and she was never called to testify before the Warren Commission.

Johnny-on-the-Spot

He was the manager of a shoe store in the Oak Cliff neighborhood of Dallas. Johnny Calvin Brewer was listening to news reports about the assassination when he heard reports that a police officer had just been killed a few blocks away. A man whose behavior seemed suspicious then walked into the shoe store. Brewer said the man stared at the display in the window and acted scared as police cars with blaring sirens raced by. After the last squad car passed, the man left the store and walked into the nearby movie theater without buying a ticket. Brewer followed, alerting the woman in the box office to call police. Once the theater lights went on, Brewer pointed out the suspicious man seated in the fifth seat from the aisle in the third to last row. Oswald was arrested after a brief scuffle, during which he punched an officer and pulled a gun.

Theater of War

Cry of Battle, starring Van Heflin and Rita Moreno, was the movie playing on a double-bill at the Texas Theater when Lee Harvey Oswald was arrested. The other half of the double feature, *War Is Hell*, had been held from U.S. release for almost three years because of what was claimed by some to be anti-American content.

100,000,000,000,000,000 to 1

In the three-year period that followed the murder of President Kennedy, 18 material witnesses died – six by gunfire, three in motor accidents, two by suicide, one from a cut throat, one from a karate chop to the neck, three from heart attacks and two from natural causes. An actuary, engaged by the *London Sunday Times*, concluded that on November 22, 1963, the odds against these witnesses being dead by February 1967 were one hundred thousand trillion to one.

Convenient Death

During her 35-year career as a gossip columnist, crime reporter and panelist on the weekly TV game show, "What's My Line?," Dorothy Kilgallen was a fearless journalist who broke major stories, and was the only reporter to interview Lee Harvey Oswald's killer, Jack Ruby. In 1965 Kilgallen began to tell friends that she was close to discovering who assassinated Kennedy, and according to David Welsh of *Ramparts Magazine*, she vowed she would "crack this case." She died mysteriously in November 1965, after being threatened, but the police never probed further. As the cause of her death was officially ruled "undetermined," some believe that Kilgallen was murdered in order to silence her.

Such Good Friends

George de Mohrenschildt emigrated from Russia to the United States in May 1938 and became a respected member of the Russian émigré community in Dallas. He became acquainted with both George H. W. Bush and Jacqueline Bouvier Kennedy (when she was still a child). During the summer of 1962, de Mohrenschildt befriended Lee Harvey Oswald and maintained that friendship until Oswald's death, insisting that Oswald had been a scapegoat in the assassination. On March 29, 1977, he received a business card from an investigator for the House Committee on Assassinations, requesting an interview. That afternoon, he was found dead from a shotgun blast to the head. The coroner's verdict was suicide.

SS-100-X

The presidential limousine, a 1961 Lincoln Continental, code named SS-100-X, was modified to Secret Service specifications by Ford Motor Company's Advanced Vehicles Group, assisted by coachbuilder Hess & Eisenhardt of Cincinnati, Ohio. Together, these two companies created a parade limousine that cost the government $200,000. The car was painted in a special shade of midnight blue, and was equipped with a hand-built 350-horsepower 430 cubic inch engine; the wheelbase was extended from the stock 133 to 156 inches, with the additional length being added between the front and rear doors and just beyond the rear doors. Following the assassination, the car was sent back to Hess & Eisenhardt to be modified further, and was rebuilt from the ground up. It continued to serve Lyndon Johnson until 1967 and remained in service for less important duties until 1978, when it was retired to the Henry Ford Museum.

Bubble Trouble

The term "bubble-top" became widely used to describe the removable top, although it was much more than a clear "bubble" over the President's car; it was a very formal design with a vinyl covering, which transformed the convertible into a limousine with a very small rear window. The vehicle was notorious for its inadequate cooling of the rear of the passenger cabin while the bubble top was in place, particularly in sunshine. In order to prevent excessive heat and discomfort to passengers, the bubble-top was often removed prior to parades, as was the case in Dallas on November 22nd. It was removed from the presidential limousine at Love Field, as requested by Secret Service agent Sam Kinney.

Home Movie

In 1941, Russian emigrant Abraham Zapruder moved to Dallas to work for Nardis, a local sportswear company. In 1949 he co-founded Jennifer Juniors, Inc., producing the Chalet and Jennifer Juniors brands. His offices were in the Dal-Tex Building, directly across the street east of the Texas School Book Depository. Not originally intending to bring his camera to work in order to film the motorcade, Zapruder, at the suggestion of his assistant, retrieved it from home before going to Dealey Plaza.

Caught on Camera

Zapruder's camera was an 8-mm Bell & Howell Zoomatic Director Series Model 414 PD – top of the line when it was purchased in 1962. Anticipating the Kennedy motorcade, Zapruder waited atop a concrete pedestal along Elm Street, his receptionist Marilyn Sitzman steadying him from behind. He began filming as the President's limousine turned onto Elm Street in front of the Book Depository, and the next 26.6 seconds were captured on 486 frames of Kodak Kodachrome II 8-mm safety film. Zapruder assumed the gunfire came from behind him because the President's head went backwards from the fatal shot, and because police officers ran to the area behind him.

Candid Cameras

In the 12 years that followed the assassination, the general public never saw the now-famous footage of Kennedy's death shot by Abraham Zapruder. At most, they had seen only selected frames as published in *Life* magazine and republished elsewhere. Not until 1975 did the general public get to see the full footage, when it was broadcast during an ABC special. A wave of outrage ensued, leading to criticism of ABC for broadcasting something so graphic. Although the film shot by Abraham Zapruder is the most famous footage of the assassination, many other cameras – both motion and single-frame – were in use that day in Dealey Plaza. Researchers have accounted for at least 32 of them.

Never Before Revealed

The Zapruder film was first shown to the public during a March 1975 broadcast of *Goodnight America*, hosted by Geraldo Rivera. Almost immediately, with the film showing a backward snap of President Kennedy's head, indicating to many a shot from the right front and hence a conspiracy, there were new demands for a re-investigation. The findings of the Rockefeller Commission that year and the Church Committee the following year added impetus to calls for a new inquiry, which was realized by the House Select Committee on Assassinations from 1977 to 1979. That investigation concluded President Kennedy "was probably assassinated as a result of a conspiracy."

Nix Fix Stix

Orville Orhel Nix was an air conditioning engineer working for the General Services Administration in Dallas. On the day of the assassination, he filmed the motorcade as it entered the Plaza, then quickly moved to the south curb of Main Street. Key to the film's significance is the photographer's perspective from the south curb of Main Street inside Dealey Plaza – the reverse angle from the Abraham Zapruder film – showing the grassy knoll in the background. After learning that the FBI would be interested in obtaining any film relating to the assassination, Nix delivered his film to the local office in Dallas. It was returned to him three days later with frames missing from the film. Nix always maintained he heard shots coming from the grassy knoll.

Snakes in the Grass

Just two days before the President's murder, suspicious activity caught the eyes of two Dallas policemen on routine patrol in Dealey Plaza. The officers observed men with rifles standing behind the picket fence on the plaza's grassy knoll. The riflemen, perhaps participating in mock target practice, were aiming their guns over the fence in the direction of the street. By the time the patrolmen reached the area, the unidentified men had vanished.

Black Dog Man

Many witnesses claim they heard shots coming from the grassy knoll on the north side of Elm Street. Photos taken of the area on the day of the assassination show a mysterious silhouette resembling a black dog leaning on the fence at the top of the grassy knoll, hence the nickname "Black Dog Man." No one ever came forward to say they were there that day, leaning on the fence at that location.

The Man Who Wasn't There

Minutes before the assassination, Gordon L. Arnold was moving toward the railroad bridge over the triple underpass to take movie film of the presidential motorcade when, he explained, "this guy just walked towards me and said that I shouldn't be up there." Arnold challenged the man's authority, he said, and the man "showed me a badge and said he was with the Secret Service and that he didn't want anybody up there." Dallas Policeman Joe Marshall Smith described encountering a Secret Service agent on the grassy knoll where many witnesses heard gunfire, but it has been established that not only were there no Secret Service agents stationed on or behind the grassy knoll, but there were no FBI or other federal agents stationed there either. On August 27, 1978, *The Dallas Morning News* published an article by Earl Golz alleging that several "counterfeit" agents of the Secret Service were in Dealey Plaza shortly before and after the assassination.

Badge Man

As the presidential motorcade passed through Dealey Plaza, Mary Moorman took a series of photographs with her Polaroid camera. Her nonprofessional photos captured images of all of the presidential limousine occupants, several other close witnesses (including Abraham Zapruder filming), two Dallas police motorcycle presidential escorts, and much of the Plaza's grassy knoll. One image seemed to depict the head and shoulders of a man behind the stockade fence, in a stance possibly consistent with the firing of a rifle, his face partly obscured by a white image that could be interpreted as a muzzle flash or smoke from a rifle. He has been described as a person wearing some kind of police uniform, and his moniker, "Badge Man," derives from a bright spot on the chest, said to resemble a gleaming badge.

Lady in Red

Norma Jean Lollis Hill is known as the "Lady in Red" because of the long red raincoat she wore on the day of the assassination. She was present along with her friend Mary Moorman across from the grassy knoll, and was one of the very closest witnesses to President Kennedy when the shots were fired, only 21 feet away, leftward, and slightly behind the limousine. Hill was one of several witnesses who stated that she saw smoke lingering near the grassy knoll picket fence. In *JFK: The Last Dissenting Witness,* a 1992 biography of Jean Hill, author Bill Sloan wrote that Arlen Specter, assistant counsel for the Warren Commission, attempted to humiliate, discredit, and intimidate Hill into changing her story.

Babushka Lady

During the analysis of the Zapruder film and other footage taken that day, a mysterious woman was spotted. She was wearing a brown overcoat and a scarf on her head (a style common to Russian grandmothers called "babushkas"). The woman appeared to be holding something in front of her face which is believed to be a camera. After the shooting, she crossed Elm Street and followed the crowd that ran up the grassy knoll in search of a gunman. The police and the FBI could never find her, and the film shot from her position never turned up. In 1970, a woman named Beverly Oliver came forward and claimed to be the Babushka Lady, although her story contained many inconsistencies. She is generally regarded as a fraud.

Umbrella Man

A person dubbed "The Umbrella Man" has been the object of much speculation, as he was the only person seen carrying and opening an umbrella on that sunny day. He stood on the sidewalk as the President was about to pass, opened an umbrella, and rotated the open umbrella while standing under it, as if somehow tracking the President with it as the limousine approached. He pumped the umbrella up and down, as if signaling, right after Kennedy is first shot. And after more shots have been fired, fatally wounding the President, and while everyone else is running about or fearfully lying low on the plaza grass, the man with the umbrella calmly lowers and closes it. Then he and another man, with chaos all around them, casually sit down together on the curb.

The Three Tramps

Three men discovered in a boxcar in the rail yard west of the grassy knoll after the assassination became known as the "three tramps." Despite the Dallas Police Department's lack of evidence connecting them to the assassination, some researchers have continued to speculate that they may have been connected to the crime. Photographs of the men at their time of arrest has fueled speculation as to their identities as they appeared to be well-dressed and clean-shaven, seemingly unlikely hobos riding the rails. Some researchers also thought it suspicious that the Dallas police had quickly released the tramps from custody apparently without investigating whether they might have witnessed anything significant related to the assassination, and that police claimed to have lost the records of their arrests as well as their mugshots and fingerprints.

Power Elite

Leroy Fletcher Prouty served as Chief of Special Operations for the Joint Chiefs of Staff under President Kennedy. Prouty has written that he believes the assassination was a coup d'etat, and that there is a secret, global "power elite" which operates covertly to protect its interests – and in doing so has frequently subverted democracy around the world. According to Prouty, people within the intelligence and military communities of the government conspired to assassinate Kennedy. He believes that the assassination was orchestrated by C.I.A. agent Edward Lansdale and that Landsdale appears in photographs of the "three tramps." According to Prouty, the movement of Kennedy after a bullet struck his head was consistent with a shot from the grassy knoll.

Turning a Blind Eye

Any witness statements that pointed to a conspiracy were ignored by the Warren Commission. In 1967, Josiah Thompson, author of *Six Seconds in Dallas: A Micro-Study of the Kennedy Assassination*, stated that the Commission ignored the testimony of seven witnesses who saw gunsmoke in the area of the stockade fence on the grassy knoll, as well as an eighth witness who smelled gunpowder at the time of the assassination. In 1989, Jim Marrs, author of *Crossfire: The Plot That Killed Kennedy*, wrote that the Commission failed to ask for the testimony of witnesses on the triple overpass whose statements pointed to a shooter on the grassy knoll.

Sound Effects

In 2001, a scientific study supported the conclusion first propounded by the House committee in 1979: that sounds heard on police recordings from Dealey Plaza are consistent with a shot being fired from the grassy knoll – supporting the panel's finding that Kennedy's murder probably resulted from a plot.

Secondhand Smoke

Lee Bowers operated a railroad tower that overlooked the parking lot on the north side of the grassy knoll. He reported that he saw two men behind the picket fence at the top of the grassy knoll before the shooting. After the shooting, Bowers said that one of the men remained behind the fence, and he lost track of the second man whose clothing blended into the foliage. When interviewed by Mark Lane, author of *Rush to Judgement*, Bowers noted that he saw something that attracted his attention, either a flash of light, or maybe smoke, from the knoll, leading him to believe "something out of the ordinary" had occurred there. Bowers told Lane he heard three shots, the last two in quick succession. Bowers was sure that they could not have come from the same rifle.

Taking the Blame

Kenny O'Donnell was part of what was called the "Irish mafia," the very loyal pols who had been with the Kennedys through the years. He was the chief of staff in the White House who urged a motorcade through the heart of Dallas so that JFK and Jackie could be seen by as many people as possible, and was in a car just behind the presidential limousine when Kennedy was shot. He was a World War II veteran. He knew gunfire. He saw where the shots came from and reported that the gunfire had come both from the grassy knoll as well as from behind. The assassination was an enormous blow to O'Donnell, who long blamed himself for the death of the President. He had a very sad life after Kennedy was killed and drank himself to death at age 53.

Bringing Up the Rear

Press photographers who normally rode in a flatbed truck directly in front of the motorcade, as they had done countless times before, were relegated to a position "out of the picture" well behind the President's limousine. According to reporter Tom Dillard, this change occurred at "the last minute" at Love Field, where two Secret Service agents, Winston G. Lawson and Roger Warner, were responsible for lining up the cars for the motorcade, including the use of numbers for the automobiles.

Inadequate and Deficient

On November 24, 1963, just hours after Oswald was fatally shot, FBI Director J. Edgar Hoover said that he wanted "something issued so we can convince the public that Oswald is the real assassin." On December 9, 1963, only 17 days after the assassination, the FBI report was issued and given to the Warren Commission. In 1979, after reviewing the FBI's investigation, the House Select Committee on Assassinations concluded that the agency failed to investigate adequately the possibility of a conspiracy and was deficient in its sharing of information with other agencies and departments.

Pabulum Digest

The Warren Commission did not include any official criminal investigators, rather it consisted of mostly elected officials including two U.S. senators, two members of the U.S. House of Representatives, and then Chief Justice of the United States, Earl Warren, along with two private citizens, all of whom relied upon government agencies to provide them with information. Richard Schweiker, United States senator and member of the Senate Select Committee on Intelligence, told author Anthony Summers in 1978, "I believe that the Warren Commission was set up at the time to feed pabulum to the American public for reasons not yet known, and that one of the biggest cover-ups in the history of our country occurred at that time."

Shoddy Craftsmanship

Robert F. Kennedy, Jr. explained that his father was gravely affected by his brother's death and spent a year contemplating the "why" and seeking understanding through reading. He explained that his father, Bobby Kennedy, did not think that a lone gunman killed President Kennedy. He said his father thought the Warren Commission, which concluded Lee Harvey Oswald acted alone in killing the president, was a "shoddy piece of craftsmanship."

Magic Bullet

Arlen Specter was appointed Philadelphia's assistant district attorney in 1959 after spending his first three years in private practice. He left the district attorney's office in 1963 to investigate the Kennedy assassination as an assistant counsel on the Warren Commission and became a household name as the Commission's chief architect. To support the group's theory that Lee Harvey Oswald acted alone, Specter developed the "single bullet theory," explaining that both Kennedy and Connally had been hit by a single shot which entered Kennedy's upper back, exited his throat, and then struck Connally, breaking a rib and shattering his wrist, and finally coming to rest in his thigh. The bullet deemed to have done all this was found somewhat mysteriously on a stretcher near an elevator in Parkland Hospital, about an hour after the victims had been brought there.

Climate of Hate

In 1961, President Kennedy appointed Sarah Tilghman Hughes to the United States District Court for the Northern District of Texas, the only female judge appointed by Kennedy and only the third woman ever to serve on the Federal bench. Two years into her tenure, she was called upon to administer the oath of office to Lyndon Johnson on Air Force One after the assassination. She remains the only woman in history to have sworn in a United States President, a task usually executed by the Chief Justice of the United States. Amid the confusion and grief of that moment, Johnson introduced her to the fallen President's widow as one of his appointees. "I loved him very much," the judge said softly to Mrs. Kennedy. Hughes later she touched off a public firestorm by excoriating the city of Dallas for the "climate of hate" in which the assassination occurred.

Photo Finish

A retired officer with the Army Signal Corps, Cecil Stoughton was the first official White House photographer. Photographers had taken pictures of presidents for more than a century before him, but only with the advent of the Kennedy administration in January 1961 was a position created for a photographer attached to the White House. Stoughton was traveling in the Kennedy motorcade in Dallas, and after shots were fired, he raced first to Parkland Hospital, then hitched a ride with a state trooper to Love Field before Air Force One took off. Police officers on the tarmac, seeing his car hurtling toward the plane and fearing another attack, nearly fired on him. Standing on a couch at the back of the plane, he took about 20 shots of the swearing-in ceremony, the only photographic record of the Johnson administration's abrupt, official beginning.

Rites of Passage

It is said that God always places you where you belong, that nothing is by accident or coincidence. Seventy-year-old Rev. Oscar L. Huber had walked the three blocks from Holy Trinity Catholic Church where he served as pastor to watch President Kennedy's motorcade pass along the parade route. The priest thought that Kennedy noticed his Roman collar and waved to him; after the motorcade was out of sight, he returned to the parish rectory. Hearing that Kennedy had been shot, he got into a car and drove to Parkland Hospital, where he administered the last rites of the Roman Catholic Church to the mortally wounded president.

Badgering the Witness

Malcolm Oliver Perry was the first doctor to attend to President Kennedy at Parkland Hospital, performing a tracheotomy over the small wound in Kennedy's throat and administering closed chest massage. "We never had any hope of saving his life," said Dr. Perry, who also rendered aid to Governor Connally. Perry stated three times at a press conference later that day that Kennedy's neck wound appeared to be an entrance wound, however, Secret Service agent Elmer Moore "badgered" Perry into changing his initial (and firm) diagnosis that the throat wound was an entrance wound.

Time Change

If the doctors were ready to declare Kennedy dead at 12:50 PM, why then was the official time listed as 1 PM? The time of death, it seems, was a fiction created to satisfy Mrs. Kennedy. According to Catholic doctrine, the last rites had to be delivered before the soul left the body. If her husband was already officially dead before Father Huber had a chance to administer the sacrament, it would not have been valid. "Father, do you think the sacrament had effect," she asked Huber in the emergency room. He tried to ally her fears. "I am convinced that his soul had not left his body," he said. "This was a valid last sacrament."

Stealing the Body

At Parkland Hospital, as the Secret Service and the President's aides wheeled his bronze casket towards the exit, they were stopped by Dr. Earl Rose, the medical examiner for Dallas County who informed the men that Texas state law required that an autopsy in a murder be performed in the county where the crime had taken place. Roy Kellerman, head of the White House Secret Service detail, squared off against Rose. Obscenities were shouted. Unconfirmed accounts said Kellerman pointed a gun at Rose. The medical examiner, the Justice of the Peace, and several Dallas policemen were forcibly shoved aside. In a 1992 interview, Rose said that an autopsy performed in Dallas "would have been free of any perceptions of outside influence."

No Experience Necessary

The autopsy of President Kennedy was performed, beginning at about 8 PM and ending at about Midnight EST, on the day of his assassination, at the Bethesda Naval Hospital in Bethesda, Maryland. Commander James J. Humes, Director of Laboratories of the National Medical School, officially conducted the autopsy. His first assistant was Commander J. Thornton Boswell, Chief of Pathology at the Naval Medical School. Humes and Boswell were hospital administrators and had never performed an autopsy in their medical careers. At the conclusion of the autopsy, Humes destroyed his notes as well as the first draft of the autopsy report.

Disguise and Deception

In his 1981 book, *Best Evidence*, David Lifton explains the discrepancy in medical reporting between Dallas and Bethesda as due to alteration of the President's body prior to autopsy. He speculates that Kennedy's body had been altered between the Dallas hospital and the autopsy site at Bethesda for the purpose of creating erroneous conclusions about the number and direction of the shots. He details evidence – using both Warren Commission documents and original research and interviews with those involved at both Dallas and Bethesda – of a stark and radical change between the descriptions of the wounds by the medical staff at Dallas and those at Bethesda.

The Missing Physician

Assistant White House Physician, Admiral George Burkley rode in the Dallas motorcade, was present at Parkland Hospital, rode Air Force One to Washington with the President's body, and was present at the autopsy. Burkley was never interviewed by the Warren Commission despite being the only physician capable of resolving clear discrepancies between the medical reports from Parkland and the Bethesda autopsy.

Altered Images

In a sworn interview, Saundra Kay Spencer, the technician at the Navy's photographic laboratory who developed Kennedy's autopsy photos, insisted that the photos in the National Archives are not the ones she developed. Those she had worked with, she said, had "no blood or opening cavities." Spencer theorized that a second photographer took pictures of a cleaned-up corpse and speculated that was done at the request of the Kennedy family in case autopsy pictures had to be made public. "Between those photographs and the ones we did," said Spencer, "there had to be some massive cosmetic things done to the President's body."

Death Announcement

Malcolm MacGregor "Mac" Kilduff was Kennedy's Assistant White House Press Secretary, the ranking Press Secretary on Kennedy's trip to Dallas (the main White House press secretary, Pierre Salinger, was traveling to Japan with six members of the Cabinet). It fell to Kilduff to bring the news from Kennedy's trauma room to Vice President Johnson waiting in another room in the hospital. Kilduff walked up to Johnson and addressed him as "Mr. President," as Lady Bird Johnson let out a short scream. Kilduff asked for Johnson's approval to announce Kennedy's death to the public, but Johnson ordered that the announcement be made only after he left the hospital. Once he received confirmation that Johnson was back at Air Force One, Kilduff announced President Kennedy's death to the press assembled in a nurse's classroom at Parkland Hospital.

Don't Quote Me

White House press man Malcolm Kilduff told reporters at Parkland Hospital that afternoon that Dr. Burkley told him a bullet entered the right temple, and Kilduff pointed to his own right temple to illustrate the trajectory. This was all captured on film. One of the reporters who attended that press conference wrote in his notes "bullet entered right temple." In a 1967 oral history, Burkley was asked whether he agreed with the Warren Commission's view on the number of shots. Burkley's reply: "I would not care to be quoted on that."

Broadcast News

The media often describe the Kennedy assassination and the coverage that followed it as the birth of modern television news. The story was covered for four days straight, night and day, beginning Friday afternoon and not returning to other programming until Tuesday. In the end, the assassination set off an unprecedented stretch of news coverage that remained unmatched for 38 years – until the terrorist attacks of September 11, 2001.

Perfect Patsy

Soon after his capture, Oswald declared, "I didn't shoot anybody" and, "They've taken me in because of the fact that I lived in the Soviet Union. I'm just a patsy!" (Oswald has been suspected of being a member of the C.I.A.'s so-called fake defector program, which was set up in the 1950s as a way to send spies into the USSR). Interrogated several times during his two days at Dallas Police Headquarters, Oswald denied killing Kennedy and Tippit, denied owning a rifle, and said two photographs of him holding a rifle and a pistol were fakes. President Johnson on Lee Harvey Oswald: "He was quite a mysterious fellow, and he did have a connection . . . The extent of the influence of those connections on him I think history will deal with more than we're able to now."

The Fritz Blitz

John Will Fritz was the first person to question suspected assassin Lee Harvey Oswald just hours after Kennedy was shot. After completing a marathon interrogation of Oswald, Fritz was told that there was a call holding for him from the White House. On the line, the newly installed President, Lyndon Johnson, reportedly told Fritz, "You've got your man, now we'll take it from here." A short while later, the FBI seized full control of the most famous murder investigation in U.S. history.

Cutout for the Job

On the night of his arrest, Oswald attempted to place a call to a man named John Hurt in Raleigh, North Carolina, but was mysteriously prevented from completing the call. Hurt was a former member of the intelligence community, and some have speculated that he was Oswald's "cutout" (In espionage parlance, a cutout is someone who is a go-between who really isn't a part of any operation or know the people involved, he just gets people in touch with other people.) Oswald seemed to be following standard procedure for a C.I.A. asset under duress.

The "Assassin's" Assassin

On Sunday, November 24, Oswald was being led through the basement of Dallas Police Headquarters in advance of his transfer to the county jail. At 11:21 AM, Jack Ruby stepped from the crowd and fired one shot into his left lower chest. The round struck several organs, penetrated his stomach, and tore his vena cava and aorta. Oswald was rushed unconscious to Parkland Memorial Hospital – the same hospital where doctors tried to save President Kennedy's life two days earlier. Oswald was pronounced dead at 1:07 PM. Ruby, who operated a local strip joint called the Carousel, had minor connections to organized crime. He features prominently in assassination theories, and many believe he killed Oswald to keep him from revealing a larger conspiracy. In his trial, Ruby denied the allegation and pleaded innocent on the grounds that his great grief over Kennedy's murder had caused him to suffer "psychomotor epilepsy" and shoot Oswald unconsciously.

Last Words

Wearing a Texas-made Resistol cowboy hat, Dallas homicide detective Jim Leavelle was handcuffed to Oswald as he was escorted through the basement of Dallas Police headquarters. In a 2006 interview, Leavelle, who helped to interrogate Oswald after his arrest, recalled joking to Oswald before the transfer, "Lee, if anybody shoots at you, I hope they're as good a shot as you are." He kind of smiled and said, "Nobody's going to shoot at me.

Breaking News

An estimated fifty journalists were in the basement of the city jail, waiting to report the transfer of Oswald. As one participant recalled, "All the newsmen were poking their sound mikes across to him and asking questions, and they were everyone sticking their flashbulbs up and around and over (Oswald) and his face." The "near-blinding television and motion picture lights which were allowed to shine upon the escort party increased the difficulty of observing unusual movements in the basement." This would later give rise to discussions about whether journalists had facilitated Oswald's death.

No Smoking Gun

The first reports from the sixth floor of the Texas School Book Depository indicated that a 7.5 German Mauser was found; by the final report, the murder weapon had morphed into a 6.5 Mannlicher Carcano. On November 5, 1969, Dallas Police Chief Jesse Curry was quoted by United Press International: "We don't have any proof that Oswald fired the rifle. No one has been able to put him in that building with a gun in his hand."

Broken Taps

Sergeant Keith Clark, as lead trumpeter in the Army Band, was assigned the task of sounding taps at the President's funeral at Arlington National Cemetery. Clark had played taps daily for four years, giving hundreds of flawless performances at Arlington and adjacent Fort Myer. At Kennedy's funeral, Clark swallowed hard as the 21 guns fired, then took his cue. On the sixth note, he faltered, then went on to complete taps without another flaw. His imperfect rendition of taps came to be seen as the embodiment of national sorrow. In his book, *The Death of a President*, William Manchester wrote how the broken note "was like a catch in your voice, or a swiftly stifled sob."

"Black Jack"

President Kennedy's flag-draped casket was moved from the White House to the Capitol on a caisson drawn by six grey horses, accompanied by a riderless horse named "Black Jack," a half-Morgan named for General of the Armies John "Black Jack" Pershing. At Mrs. Kennedy's request, the cortege and other ceremonial details were modeled on the funeral of Abraham Lincoln. Crowds lined Pennsylvania Avenue and many wept openly as the caisson passed. During the 21 hours that the President's body lay in state in the Capitol Rotunda, about 250,000 people filed by to pay their respects.

Into the Deep

After Kennedy was declared dead at Parkland Hospital in Dallas, his body was wrapped in sheets and placed into a heavy, ornate, solid-bronze casket with white satin lining for the flight back to Washington; he was later buried in a mahogany casket in Arlington National Cemetery after it was discovered the bronze casket had been damaged and was missing a handle. The original casket was loaded with three 80-pound bags of sand, drilled with holes and loaded into a pine box that was also drilled full of holes. It was dumped in the Atlantic Ocean from a military aircraft above an area used to dispose of unstable and outdated weapons.

Final Resting Place

On March 3, 1963, while touring Arlington National Cemetery, President Kennedy remarked: "The view up here is so beautiful. I could stay here forever." Kennedy is one of only two American presidents buried at Arlington (the other is William Howard Taft, who died in 1930). Lighted by Mrs. Kennedy during the funeral, an "eternal flame" burns from the center of a five-foot circular flat-granite stone at the head of the grave. The burner is a specially designed apparatus created by the Institute of Gas Technology of Chicago. A constantly flashing electric spark near the tip of the nozzle relights the gas should the flame be extinguished by rain, wind or accident. The fuel is natural gas and is mixed with a controlled quantity of air to achieve the color and shape of the flame.

Grave Injustice

Lee Harvey Oswald was buried in Shannon Rose Hill Cemetery in Fort Worth, Texas on November 25, 1963, the same day John F. Kennedy was interred at Arlington. The marker is plain: OSWALD. No first name, no date of birth, no date of death. His original grave marker was stolen and cemetery workers are now told not to give directions to his plot.

Artifacts

The plane serving JFK as Air Force One is on display at the National Museum of the United States Air Force in Dayton, Ohio where tours of the aircraft are offered, including the rear of the aircraft where Kennedy's casket was placed and the location where Lyndon Johnson was sworn in as President. The 1961 Lincoln Continental limousine is at the Henry Ford Museum in Dearborn, Michigan. Equipment from the trauma room at Parkland Memorial Hospital, including a gurney, was purchased by the federal government from Parkland Hospital in 1973 and stored at an underground facility in Lenexa, Kansas. The First Lady's pink suit, the autopsy report and X-rays, rifle used by Oswald, his diary, bullet fragments, and the limousine windshield are stored in the National Archives facility in College Park, Maryland.

"X" Marks the Spot

Although Elm Street is still an active city street, the spot where the presidential limousine was located at the time of the shooting is marked with an X on the street.

Curious George

George E. Joannides was the C.I.A. case officer who oversaw dissident Cubans in 1963 and had dealings with Lee Harvey Oswald in the run-up to the assassination. In 1978, the agency made Joannides the liaison to the House Select Committee on Assassinations – but never told the committee of his earlier role. That concealment has fueled suspicion that Mr. Joannides' real assignment was to limit what the House committee could learn about C.I.A. activities. According to committee counsel G. Robert Blakey, "He was put in a position to edit everything we were given before it was given to us."

The Garrison Goosechase

Earling Carothers "Jim" Garrison was the District Attorney of Orleans Parish, Louisiana, who began an investigation into the assassination of President Kennedy in late 1966, leading to the arrest and trial of businessman Clay Shaw in 1969, with Shaw being unanimously acquitted less than one hour after the case went to the jury. In a 1992 interview, Edward Haggerty, who was the judge at the trial, stated: "I believe he (Shaw) was lying to the jury. Of course, the jury probably believed him. But I think Shaw put a good con job on the jury." Opinions differ as to whether Garrison uncovered a conspiracy behind the assassination, but was blocked from successful prosecution by a federal government cover-up, whether he bungled his chance to uncover a conspiracy, or whether the entire case was an unproductive waste of resources.

What the Polls Say

In 1964, after the release of the Warren Report, the U.S. government's official version of the assassination, a CBS poll found that more than 40 percent of Americans surveyed said there was more to the assassination than the government had revealed. In 1976, a Gallup Poll found that 81 percent believed in a conspiracy. A recent CBS survey found that 90 percent of Americans reject the Warren Commission's conclusions.

Coup d'état

An article concerning Kennedy's relationship with the CIA was written by journalist Arthur Krock, and published in *The New York Times* on October 3, 1963. The article, entitled "The Intra-Administration War in Vietnam," quotes a high-ranking official in the government as saying "the CIA's growth was likened to a malignancy" which this "very high official was not even sure the White House could control ... any longer. If the United States ever experiences (an attempt at a coup to overthrow the government) it will come from the CIA and not the Pentagon." The "agency represents a tremendous power and total unaccountability to anyone."

Blowin' in the Wind

The CIA had a number of high profile conflicts with the President, despite the fact that his brother, Attorney General Robert Kennedy, had effective authority over the Agency. Kennedy's relationship with the CIA was strained considerably following the failed Bay of Pigs Invasion. He remarked that he wanted "to splinter the CIA into a thousand pieces and scatter it to the winds."

Conspiracy of Tycoons

Jacqueline Kennedy believed that Lyndon Johnson and a cabal of Texas tycoons were involved in the assassination of her husband. In his book, *Brothers, the Hidden History of the Kennedy Years*, David Talbot discovered that Robert Kennedy felt he had pieced together the assassination conspiracy within weeks of the murder. Bobby called Jackie and the family together to reveal his findings. He said that the CIA and the military carried out the execution with the involvement of what we might now call Texas oil oligarchs.

Hunt for Truth

Shortly before his death in 2007, Howard Hunt authored an autobiography which implicated Lyndon Johnson in the assassination, suggesting that Johnson had orchestrated the killing with the help of CIA agents who had been angered by Kennedy's actions as President. A 2007 article published in *Rolling Stone* magazine revealed deathbed confessions by Hunt to his son which suggested a conspiracy to kill President Kennedy by Johnson, CIA agents Cord Meyer, Bill Harvey and David Sánchez Morales, and an unnamed "French gunman," who purportedly shot at Kennedy from the grassy knoll.

French Connection

According to a CIA document released in 1977, Jean Soutre, member of a right-wing extremist group, the OAS (Organisation de l'Armée Secrète), was in Dallas on November 22, 1963. Soutre, or a man claiming to be him, was detained by U.S. authorities in Texas and deported within forty-eight hours of the shooting.

The Mob's Greatest Hit?

David E. Scheim has published two books claiming that the Mafia were responsible for the Kennedy assassination. He believes that it was organized by Carlos Marcello, Santos Trafficante and Jimmy Hoffa. This theory is based on the idea that the Mafia were angry with both John and Robert Kennedy for their attempts to destroy organized crime. Scheim's theory was supported by Trafficante's lawyer, Frank Ragano, who published the book *Mob Lawyer*, in 1994. In 1992, the nephew of Sam Giancana published *Double Cross: The Story of the Man Who Controlled America*. The book attempted to establish that Giancana had rigged the 1960 Presidential election vote in Cook County on John Kennedy's behalf, which effectively gave Kennedy the election. It is argued that Kennedy reneged on the deal and therefore Giancana had him killed.

"They're After Us All"

A 1978 interview with Brigadier General Godfrey McHugh, President Kennedy's military aide on the Dallas trip, remained closed for 31 years, but was finally declassified in 2009, revealing an incident on Air Force One. After the assassination, as the plane was preparing to return to Washington, McHugh encountered Lyndon Johnson "hiding in the toilet in the bedroom compartment and muttering, 'Conspiracy, conspiracy, they're after all of us.'"

Unsolved Mystery

To date, there is no consensus on who, among many possible players, may have been involved in a conspiracy to kill President Kennedy. Those often mentioned as being part of a conspiracy include Jack Ruby, organized crime as an organization or organized crime individuals, the CIA, the FBI, the Secret Service, the KGB, right-wing groups or right-wing individuals, President Lyndon Johnson, pro- or anti-Castro Cubans, the military and/or industrial groups allied with the military.

Lock Box

In 1964, President Lyndon Johnson signed Executive Order No. 11652, which ordered evidence related to the Kennedy assassination locked up in the National Archives until the year 2039.

BIBLIOGRAPHY

Brauer, Carl. *John F. Kennedy and the Second Reconstruction* (1977)

Burner, David. *John F. Kennedy and a New Generation* (1988)

Collier, Peter and Horowitz, David. *The Kennedys* (1984)

Cottrell, John. *Assassination! The World Stood Still* (1964)

Douglass, James W. *JFK and the Unspeakable: Why He Died and Why It Matters* (2008)

Fay, Paul B., Jr. *The Pleasure of His Company* (1966)

Garrison, Jim. *On the Trail of the Assassins* (1988)

Giglio, James. *The Presidency of John F. Kennedy* (1991)

Groden, Robert J. and Livingstone, Harrison. *High Treason* (1990)

Groden, Robert J. *The Killing of a President* (1993)

Harper, Paul, and Krieg, Joann P. eds. *John F. Kennedy: The Promise Revisited* (1988)

Heath, Jim F. *Decade of Disillusionment: The Kennedy-Johnson Years* (1976)

Hellmann, John. *The Kennedy Obsession: The American Myth of JFK* (1997)

Hersh, Seymour. *The Dark Side of Camelot* (1997)

Hughes, B. *The Secret Terrorists* (2002)

Hughes, B. *The Enemy Unmasked* (2006)

Kunz, Diane B. *The Diplomacy of the Crucial Decade: American Foreign Relations during the 1960s* (1994)

Lane, Mark. *Plausible Denial* (1991)

Lifton, David. *Best Evidence* (1988)

Lynch, Grayston L. *Decision for Disaster: Betrayal at the Bay of Pigs* (2000)

Manchester, William. *Portrait of a President: John F. Kennedy in Profile* (1967)
Manchester, William (1967). *The Death of a President* (1963)
Marrs, Jim. *Crossfire* (1989)
Newman, John M. *JFK and Vietnam: Deception, Intrigue, and the Struggle for Power* (1992)
North, Mark. *Act of Treason* (1991)
Parmet, Herbert. *Jack: The Struggles of John F. Kennedy* (1980)
Parmet, Herbert. *JFK: The Presidency of John F. Kennedy* (1983
Reeves, Thomas. *A Question of Character: A Life of John F. Kennedy* (1991
Scheim, David E. *Contract on America* (1983)
Summers, Anthony. *Conspiracy* (1989)
Wills, Garry. *The Kennedy Imprisonment* (1981)
Zelizer, Barbie. *Covering the Body* (1992)

In Invitation

With a view to future revisions, suggestions for additions, corrections of errors, or changes in biographical data are invited.

The publishers cordially invite you to submit your criticisms of this book and any other volumes that bear the History Company name. Ideas for new books or reprints to be added to our catalogue are also most welcome.

Please address your criticisms, corrections,
or suggestions to:
support@historycompany.com

Made in United States
Orlando, FL
16 March 2025